Bedtime Stories

for Babies, Toddlers and Kids

Colorfull Brothers

Copyright © 2023 di Colorfull Brothers.

All rights reserved. No part of this book may be used or reproduced in any form without written permission, except for brief quotations in critical articles or reviews.

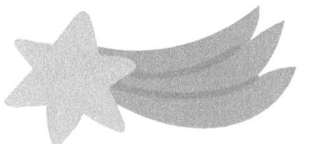

Table of Contents

The butterfly Luci…………………………………..5

The teddy bear Birba………………………………..7

The king and the child……………………………..9

The hare and the bear……………………………..11

The fairy and the unhappy king……………..15

The princess and the wandering prince…17

The royalty of the wolf princess……………20

The adventure of the little bear……………..23

Table of Contents

The bunny named Salta........................26

The Little Pio Chick..........................28

The kitten Molly..............................30

The mouse Tino and the fox.................32

The adventure of the little unicorn 34

Little Bear Bruno.............................37

This book belongs to:

....

The butterfly Luci

ONCE UPON A TIME THERE WAS A LITTLE BUTTERFLY NAMED LUCI WHO LIVED IN A GARDEN FULL OF FLOWERS. LUCI LOVED TO FLY AMONG THE FLOWERS AND ADMIRE ALL THEIR COLORS AND SCENTS. ONE DAY, AS SHE WAS FLYING FROM ONE FLOWER TO ANOTHER, SHE MET AN OLD LADYBUG WHO ASKED HER, "WHERE ARE YOU GOING, LITTLE BUTTERFLY?"
LUCI REPLIED, "I AM FLYING FROM ONE FLOWER TO ANOTHER TO ADMIRE ALL THEIR COLORS AND SCENTS!"
THE OLD LADYBUG SMILED AND TOLD HER, "YOU KNOW, THE FLOWERS HAVE A SECRET THAT THEY WANT TO SHARE ONLY WITH THE BRAVEST BUTTERFLIES. IF YOU WANT TO KNOW THIS SECRET, YOU MUST FLY TO THE CENTER OF THE GARDEN AND LOOK INTO THE HEART OF THE LARGEST FLOWER."

LUCI DID NOT HESITATE FOR A MOMENT AND FLEW TO THE CENTER OF THE GARDEN. WHEN HE REACHED THE LARGEST FLOWER, HE LOOKED INTO ITS HEART AND SAW THAT THE SECRET WAS A WONDERFUL RAINBOW OF LIGHTS.

AND SO, EVERY NIGHT, LUCI DREAMED OF FLYING THROUGH THE RAINBOW OF LIGHTS AND ALWAYS DISCOVERING NEW WONDERS. AND EVERY DAY, WHEN SHE WOKE UP, SHE WAS BRAVER AND FULL OF JOY.

AND THIS IS THE END OF THE STORY. GOOD NIGHT, LITTLE LISTENER, SWEET DREAMS AND DREAMS OF FLYING THROUGH THE RAINBOW OF LIGHTS!

The teddy bear Birba

ONCE UPON A TIME THERE WAS A LITTLE BEAR NAMED BIRBA WHO LIVED IN A CABIN IN THE FOREST. BIRBA LOVED FISHING, PLAYING WITH HIS ANIMAL FRIENDS AND DREAMING OF ADVENTURES. ONE DAY, WHILE FISHING IN A RIVER, HE MET AN OLD WOLF WHO ASKED HIM, "WHAT ARE YOU DOING, LITTLE BEAR?" BIRBA REPLIED, "I'M FISHING TO HAVE DINNER WITH MY FRIENDS TONIGHT!" THE OLD WOLF SMILED AND TOLD HIM, "YOU KNOW, BEYOND THIS FOREST IS A WORLD FULL OF ADVENTURES WAITING FOR YOU. IF YOU WANT TO EXPERIENCE IT, YOU MUST HAVE THE COURAGE TO EXPLORE AND NOT BE AFRAID TO DISCOVER NEW THINGS."
BIRBA WAS VERY CURIOUS AND DECIDED TO FOLLOW THE OLD WOLF'S ADVICE. HE SET OUT TO DISCOVER THE WORLD TOGETHER WITH HIS MOST LOYAL FRIENDS, A RABBIT AND A MONKEY.

DURING THE JOURNEY THEY ENCOUNTERED MANY OTHER ANIMALS, SOME FRIENDLY AND SOME LESS SO. BUT BIRBA WAS NOT INTIMIDATED, AND WITH HER COURAGE AND WISDOM, SHE MANAGED TO OVERCOME EVERY OBSTACLE.
THEY VISITED ENCHANTED FORESTS, TOWERING MOUNTAINS AND SANDY DESERTS, MEETING FANTASTIC CREATURES AND DISCOVERING HIDDEN TREASURES.
AND AT THE END OF THEIR JOURNEY, BIRBA AND HIS FRIENDS RETURNED TO THE FOREST WHERE THEY LIVED, RICHER IN EXPERIENCES AND ADVENTURES TO BE TOLD FOREVER.
AND EVERY NIGHT BEFORE GOING TO SLEEP, BIRBA IMAGINED WHAT OTHER ADVENTURES AWAITED HIM THE NEXT DAY.
AND THIS IS THE END OF THE STORY. GOOD NIGHT, LITTLE LISTENER, SWEET DREAMS AND DREAMS OF ADVENTURES!

The king and the child

Once upon a time there was a king who had a very special garden, with flowers of every color and trees that produced delicious fruit. The king had one wish: that his garden would always be lush and full of life.
One day, an evil sorcerer cast a spell on the garden, which suddenly began to die. All the flowers withered, the trees no longer produced fruit, and the garden became a sad and gray place.
The king, in despair, decided to offer a reward to anyone who could rid the garden of the spell. Many heroes and sorcerers tried to free the garden, but none succeeded.
One day, a very brave and curious child decided to try to free the garden. The child had no magic, but he had a pure heart and an open mind.

THE CHILD MET MANY ANIMALS IN THE GARDEN, WHO TOLD HIM ALL THE SECRETS AND LEGENDS OF THE PLACE. WITH THEIR HELP, THE CHILD DISCOVERED THAT THE SPELL COULD ONLY BE BROKEN WITH THE HELP OF A SPECIAL PLANT THAT GREW IN THE HEART OF THE GARDEN.

THE CHILD SET OUT TO FIND THE PLANT AND, DESPITE MANY DIFFICULTIES, MANAGED TO FIND IT AND BRING IT TO THE KING. WITH THE PLANT, THE KING WAS ABLE TO BREAK THE SPELL, AND THE GARDEN BECAME LUSH AND FULL OF LIFE AGAIN.

THE CHILD BECAME FAMOUS AS THE SAVIOR OF THE GARDEN AND WAS REWARDED WITH MANY TREASURES. BUT HE SAID THAT THE REAL REWARD HAD BEEN THE BEAUTY AND PEACE OF THE GARDEN, AND THAT HE WOULD NEVER FORGET THE FRIENDSHIPS AND ADVENTURES HE HAD HAD THERE.

AND THAT IS THE END OF THE STORY. GOOD NIGHT, LITTLE LISTENER, SWEET DREAMS AND DREAMS OF ADVENTURES!

The hare and the bear

ONCE UPON A TIME THERE WAS A SMALL AND SHY HARE WHO LIVED IN AN ENCHANTED FOREST. THE HARE LOVED THE PEACE AND QUIET OF THE FOREST VERY MUCH, BUT SOMETIMES SHE FELT LONELY AND WISHED SHE HAD A FRIEND TO PLAY WITH AND SHARE HER ADVENTURES.

ONE DAY, WHILE THE HARE WAS WALKING IN THE WOODS, SHE MET A LARGE AND CHEERFUL BEAR WHO WAS LOOKING FOR HONEY IN A TREE. THE HARE AND THE BEAR BEGAN TO TALK AND DISCOVERED THAT THEY HAD MANY THINGS IN COMMON, SUCH AS A LOVE OF PEACE AND QUIET IN THE WOODS.

THE BEAR INVITED THE HARE TO FOLLOW HIM IN HIS SEARCH FOR HONEY, AND THE HARE GLADLY ACCEPTED. TOGETHER, THEY DISCOVERED A HUGE BEEHIVE FULL OF DELICIOUS HONEY. BUT WHEN THEY TRIED TO GET SOME, THEY WERE ATTACKED BY ANGRY BEES.

THE HARE AND THE BEAR REALIZED THAT THEY NEEDED HELP AND DECIDED TO ASK THE OTHER INHABITANTS OF THE FOREST FOR HELP. TOGETHER, THEY WORKED TO PROTECT THE HIVE AND MAKE PEACE WITH THE BEES.

THROUGH THEIR COOPERATION AND FRIENDSHIP, THE HARE AND THE BEAR WERE ABLE TO GET THE HONEY AND TAKE IT HOME, WHERE THEY SHARED IT WITH THE OTHER FOREST DWELLERS.

FROM THAT DAY ON, THE HARE AND THE BEAR BECAME INSEPARABLE FRIENDS AND FELLOW ADVENTURERS, ALWAYS READY TO HELP EACH OTHER AND HAVE FUN TOGETHER.

AND THAT IS THE END OF THE STORY. GOOD NIGHT, LITTLE LISTENER, SWEET DREAMS AND DREAMS OF FRIENDSHIP!

The fairy and the unhappy king

ONCE UPON A TIME THERE WAS A KING WHO HAD A VERY LARGE AND BEAUTIFUL CASTLE WITH MANY SERVANTS AND MANY TREASURES. BUT THE KING WAS VERY DISSATISFIED BECAUSE HE HAD NO REAL FRIENDS TO SHARE HIS LIFE AND WEALTH WITH.

ONE DAY, THE KING DECIDED TO HOLD A BIG BALL TO FIND A TRUE AND SPECIAL FRIEND. HE INVITED ALL THE PRINCESSES OF THE KINGDOM, BUT NONE SEEMED SUITABLE. THEY WERE ALL BEAUTIFUL AND POLITE, BUT THE KING FELT THEY ONLY SOUGHT HIS POWER AND WEALTH.

DESPERATE, THE KING DECIDED TO GO FOR A WALK IN THE NEARBY FOREST, HOPING TO FIND SOME PEACE AND INSPIRATION. IN THE FOREST HE MET A SMALL FAIRY WHO TOLD HIM ABOUT HER DESIRE TO FIND A TRUE FRIEND.

THE FAIRY AND THE KING BEGAN TO TALK AND DISCOVERED THAT THEY HAD MANY THINGS IN COMMON.

THE FAIRY TOLD HIM ABOUT HER ADVENTURES IN THE FOREST, AND THE KING TOLD HER ABOUT HIS LIFE IN THE CASTLE.
THE KING AND THE FAIRY BECAME FRIENDS VERY QUICKLY AND DECIDED TO GO DANCING TOGETHER. WHEN THEY ARRIVED AT THE BALL, EVERYONE WAS AMAZED TO SEE THE KING WITH SUCH A SPECIAL AND BEAUTIFUL FRIEND.
THE KING AND THE FAIRY DANCED TOGETHER ALL NIGHT, LAUGHED, TALKED, AND DISCOVERED THAT THEY WERE MADE FOR EACH OTHER. AT THE END OF THE DANCE, THE KING ASKED THE FAIRY TO MARRY HIM AND BECOME HIS QUEEN.
THE FAIRY GLADLY ACCEPTED, AND THE KING AND FAIRY LIVED HAPPILY AND IN LOVE FOREVER, SHARING THEIR LIFE AND LOVE WITH ALL THE CREATURES OF THE KINGDOM. AND THAT IS THE END OF THE STORY. GOOD NIGHT, LITTLE LISTENER, SWEET DREAMS AND DREAMS OF LOVE!

The princess and the wandering prince

ONCE UPON A TIME THERE WAS A BEAUTIFUL PRINCESS WHO LIVED IN A LARGE CASTLE SURROUNDED BY A VAST KINGDOM. THE PRINCESS WAS VERY HAPPY, BUT ALSO VERY BORED, AS SHE HAD NO ONE TO PLAY WITH OR SHARE HER LIFE WITH. ONE DAY, THE PRINCESS SAW A YOUNG PRINCE WALKING THROUGH THE STREETS OF THE KINGDOM. THE PRINCE WAS VERY HANDSOME AND HAD A VERY KIND SMILE. THE PRINCESS DECIDED TO GO AND TALK TO HIM, AND IN TIME, THE TWO BECAME FRIENDS. BUT THE KINGDOM WAS THREATENED BY A TERRIBLE DRAGON WHO TERRORIZED THE PEOPLE AND DESTROYED EVERYTHING HE CAME ACROSS. THE KING OF THE KINGDOM ASKED THE WANDERING PRINCE TO HELP THEM DEFEAT THE DRAGON, AND THE PRINCE AGREED, ALTHOUGH HE WAS NOT A HERO.

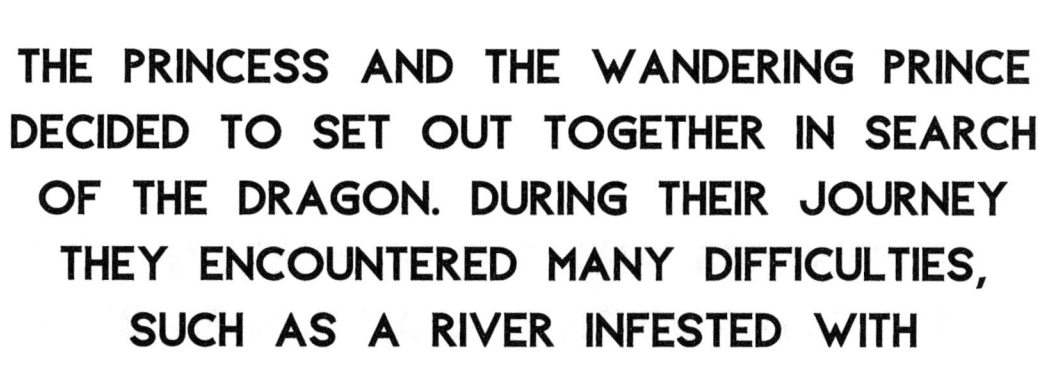

THE PRINCESS AND THE WANDERING PRINCE DECIDED TO SET OUT TOGETHER IN SEARCH OF THE DRAGON. DURING THEIR JOURNEY THEY ENCOUNTERED MANY DIFFICULTIES, SUCH AS A RIVER INFESTED WITH MONSTROUS FISH AND AN ENCHANTED FOREST POPULATED BY STRANGE AND DANGEROUS CREATURES. FINALLY, THEY ARRIVED AT THE CAVE WHERE THE DRAGON LIVED. THE PRINCESS AND THE WANDERING PRINCE DISCOVERED THAT THE DRAGON WAS NOT AN EVIL MONSTER, BUT JUST A WOUNDED ANIMAL THAT NEEDED HELP. THE PRINCESS AND THE WANDERING PRINCE DECIDED TO HELP THE DRAGON. THE PRINCESS TREATED HIS WOUNDS AND THE PRINCE FED HIM. THE DRAGON, GRATEFUL FOR THEIR HELP, DECIDED TO PROTECT THE KINGDOM FROM ENEMIES AND NEVER TO HARM ANYONE AGAIN.

THE PRINCESS AND THE WANDERING PRINCE RETURNED TO THE KINGDOM AS HEROES. THE KING AND ALL THE PEOPLE WERE HAPPY TO SEE THEM AND THANKED THE DRAGON FOR SAVING THE KINGDOM.

THE PRINCESS AND THE WANDERING PRINCE GREW OLD TOGETHER, SURROUNDED BY THE PEACE AND HAPPINESS OF THE KINGDOM. THEY BECAME LEGEND, REMEMBERED BY ALL AS THE TWO HEROES WHO HAD SAVED THE KINGDOM FROM THE THREAT OF THE DRAGON AND BROUGHT FRIENDSHIP AND LOVE TO A WORLD THAT DESPERATELY NEEDED IT.

AND SO, THE FAIRY TALE OF THE WANDERING PRINCESS AND PRINCE WAS TOLD FROM GENERATION TO GENERATION, INSPIRING CHILDREN TO BE BRAVE, GENEROUS AND KIND TO EVERYONE THEY MEET ALONG THE WAY.

The royalty of the wolf princess

IN A KINGDOM FAR AWAY, THERE WAS A WOLF PRINCESS NAMED LUNA. LUNA WAS A VERY SPECIAL PRINCESS, FOR SHE WAS A WOLF WHO HAD THE ABILITY TO TALK TO ANIMALS AND UNDERSTAND THEIR LANGUAGE. DESPITE HER UNIQUE ABILITY, LUNA WAS SAD BECAUSE HER FATHER, THE WOLF KING, WANTED HER TO ACT LIKE A TRADITIONAL PRINCESS AND STOP TALKING TO ANIMALS. LUNA COULD NOT BEAR THE IDEA OF LOSING HER SPECIAL CONNECTION WITH ANIMALS, SO SHE DECIDED TO ESCAPE THE CASTLE AND GO ON A JOURNEY TO DISCOVER THE WORLD OUTSIDE THE KINGDOM. ON HER JOURNEY, SHE MET MANY INTERESTING ANIMALS AND LEARNED MANY THINGS ABOUT HERSELF AND LIFE.

LUNA MET A GROUP OF FAIRIES WHO LIVED IN AN ENCHANTED KINGDOM. THERE, SHE LEARNED MANY THINGS ABOUT MAGIC AND THE BEAUTY OF THE WORLD AROUND HER. BUT WHEN THE FAIRY KINGDOM WAS THREATENED BY AN EVIL SORCERER, LUNA HAD TO USE HER ABILITY TO TALK TO ANIMALS AND HER INNER STRENGTH TO HELP THE FAIRIES SAVE THEIR KINGDOM. AFTER HELPING THE FAIRY KINGDOM, LUNA DECIDED IT WAS TIME TO CONFRONT HER FATHER, THE WOLF KING, AND EXPLAIN TO HIM THE IMPORTANCE OF HER ABILITY TO TALK TO ANIMALS. BUT WHEN SHE ARRIVED AT THE CASTLE, SHE DISCOVERED THAT THE WOLF KING HAD ARRANGED A CHALLENGE TO DETERMINE WHO WOULD RULE THE KINGDOM. LUNA HAD TO FACE MANY TRIALS TO PROVE HER WORTH AND HER ABILITY TO RULE AS QUEEN.

EVENTUALLY, LUNA WAS ABLE TO OVERCOME ALL THE CHALLENGES AND PROVE HER WORTH AS QUEEN. THE WOLF KING FINALLY UNDERSTOOD THE IMPORTANCE OF HER ABILITY TO TALK TO ANIMALS AND GRANTED HER PERMISSION TO RULE THE KINGDOM AS SHE SAW FIT. AND SO, LUNA BECAME THE FIRST WOLF PRINCESS TO RULE THE KINGDOM WITH WISDOM AND STRENGTH, BECOMING A ROLE MODEL FOR ALL THE PRINCES AND PRINCESSES OF THE WORLD.

The adventure of the little bear

ONCE UPON A TIME THERE WAS A LITTLE BEAR WHO LIVED IN THE WOODS WITH HIS PARENTS. HE WAS ALWAYS CURIOUS AND LOVED TO EXPLORE THE WORLD AROUND HIM. ONE DAY, HE DECIDED TO GO ON AN ADVENTURE BY HIMSELF. WHILE EXPLORING, THE LITTLE BEAR DISCOVERED A RIVER FLOWING THROUGH THE FOREST. HE WAS FASCINATED BY ALL THE CREATURES THAT LIVED IN THE RIVER AND DECIDED TO EXPLORE MORE. WHILE WALKING ALONG THE RIVER, THE LITTLE BEAR MET A FROG. THE FROG ASKED HIM WHERE HE WAS GOING, AND THE LITTLE BEAR REPLIED THAT HE WAS EXPLORING THE WORLD. THE FROG SUGGESTED THAT HE JOIN HER ON AN ADVENTURE. SO, THE LITTLE BEAR AND THE FROG BEGAN THEIR JOURNEY DOWN THE RIVER, MEETING MANY OTHER ANIMALS ALONG THE WAY. THEY ENJOYED TALKING WITH THEM AND DISCOVERING NEW THINGS.

ONE DAY, THE LITTLE BEAR AND THE FROG DISCOVERED A BIRD'S NEST HANGING FROM A TREE. INSIDE, THERE WAS A LITTLE BIRD THAT NEEDED HELP TO RETURN TO ITS MOTHER. THE LITTLE BEAR AND THE FROG DECIDED TO HELP THE LITTLE BIRD. THANKS TO THEIR FRIENDSHIP AND DETERMINATION, THE LITTLE BEAR, THE FROG AND THE LITTLE BIRD WERE ABLE TO RETURN TO THE LITTLE BIRD'S MOM. THE LITTLE BIRD'S MOTHER THANKED THEM AND GAVE THEM A KISS ON THE CHEEK. THE LITTLE BEAR LEARNED THAT FRIENDSHIP AND HELP FROM OTHERS CAN MAKE A DIFFERENCE. EVENTUALLY, THE LITTLE BEAR RETURNED TO THE FOREST WHERE HE LIVED WITH HIS PARENTS. HE TOLD THEM ALL THE THINGS HE HAD LEARNED AND DISCOVERED DURING HIS ADVENTURE AND SHARED HIS EXPERIENCE WITH THE OTHER ANIMALS IN THE WOODS. AND SO, THE LITTLE BEAR BECAME EVEN WISER AND BRAVER, AND LIVED HAPPILY EVER AFTER.

LITTLE BEAR LEARNED THAT ADVENTURE AND EXPLORATION ARE IMPORTANT FOR DISCOVERING THE WORLD AND GROWING, BUT THAT FRIENDSHIP AND HELP FROM OTHERS ARE EVEN MORE IMPORTANT. AND FROM THAT DAY ON, THE LITTLE BEAR DECIDED TO ALWAYS SHARE HIS KNOWLEDGE AND EXPERIENCE WITH THE OTHER ANIMALS IN THE FOREST.

The bunny named Salta

ONCE UPON A TIME THERE WAS A LITTLE BUNNY NAMED SALTA WHO LIVED IN A LITTLE BURROW IN THE FOREST. SALTA LOVED TO JUMP AND PLAY WITH HIS FRIENDS, BUT EVERY NIGHT BEFORE HE WENT TO SLEEP, HE WOULD STOP TO LOOK AT THE STARS AND IMAGINE FLYING AMONG THEM.

ONE DAY, WHILE HE WAS PLAYING WITH HIS FRIENDS, HE MET AN OLD SQUIRREL WHO ASKED HIM, "WHERE ARE YOU GOING, LITTLE BUNNY?"

SKIP REPLIED, "I'M GOING TO PLAY WITH MY FRIENDS!"

THE OLD SQUIRREL SMILED AND TOLD HIM, "SEE THOSE STARS UP THERE? EACH ONE OF THEM REPRESENTS AN ADVENTURE YOU CAN HAVE IF ONLY YOU WISH. DREAM OF FLYING AMONG THEM EVERY NIGHT AND YOU WILL SEE THAT THE ADVENTURES WILL BECOME MORE AND MORE REAL."

SKIP FOLLOWED THE OLD SQUIRREL'S ADVICE AND FROM THAT DAY ON, EVERY NIGHT BEFORE HE WENT TO SLEEP, HE DREAMED OF FLYING AMONG THE STARS. AND EVERY NIGHT, HIS DREAMS BECAME MORE AND MORE VIVID AND REAL.

ONE DAY, SALTA DECIDED TO SET OUT TO DISCOVER THE WORLD AND EXPERIENCE ALL THE ADVENTURES HE HAD DREAMED OF. AND SO, HE SET OUT TOWARD THE HORIZON, LEAPING AND FLYING THROUGH THE CLOUDS, HAPPY AND FULL OF JOY.

AND THAT IS THE END OF THE STORY. GOOD NIGHT, LITTLE LISTENER, SWEET DREAMS AND DREAMS OF FLYING AMONG THE STARS!

The Little Pio Chick

ONCE UPON A TIME THERE WAS A CHICK NAMED PIUS WHO LIVED IN A NEST IN THE MIDDLE OF A FIELD. PIUS LOVED TO SING AND EVERY DAY HE SANG HIS HEART OUT ALL OVER THE FIELD.

BUT ONE DAY, WHILE HE WAS SINGING, HE NOTICED THAT THE SUN WAS SETTING AND IT WAS TIME TO GO TO SLEEP. PIUS FELT A LITTLE SAD BECAUSE HE WANTED TO KEEP SINGING AND PLAYING, BUT HE KNEW IT WAS IMPORTANT TO SLEEP TO BECOME STRONG AND HEALTHY.

THEN HE DECIDED TO SING A LULLABY FOR HIMSELF AND FELL ASLEEP WITH A SMILE ON HIS LIPS. IN HIS DREAM, HE FLEW HIGH IN THE SKY TOGETHER WITH THE BIRDS AND SANG WONDERFUL SONGS.
AND THIS IS THE END OF THE STORY. GOOD NIGHT, LITTLE LISTENER, SWEET DREAMS AND DREAMS OF FLYING IN THE CLOUDS!

The kitten Molly

ONCE UPON A TIME THERE WAS A KITTEN NAMED MOLLY WHO LIVED IN A SMALL VILLAGE. MOLLY WAS A VERY CURIOUS KITTEN AND EVERY DAY HE WENT OUT TO DISCOVER THE WORLD AROUND HIM.
ONE DAY, WHILE EXPLORING THE NEARBY FOREST, MOLLY MET AN OLD MOUSE WHO ASKED HIM, "WHERE ARE YOU GOING, KITTEN?"
MOLLY REPLIED, "I AM GOING TO DISCOVER THE WORLD, I WANT TO KNOW ALL THE SECRETS IT HIDES!"

THE OLD MOUSE SMILED AND TOLD HIM, "WELL, THEN I WILL GIVE YOU A PIECE OF ADVICE. EVERY NIGHT BEFORE YOU GO TO SLEEP, STOP AND LOOK AT THE STARRY SKY AND IMAGINE THAT YOU ARE FLYING AMONG THE STARS. DREAM THAT EACH STAR REPRESENTS AN ADVENTURE YOU CAN HAVE WHEN YOU GROW UP."
MOLLY FOLLOWED THE OLD MOUSE'S ADVICE AND EVERY NIGHT BEFORE SHE WENT TO SLEEP, SHE WOULD STOP AND LOOK UP AT THE STARRY SKY. AND SO, SHE BEGAN TO DREAM OF FANTASTIC ADVENTURES AND IMAGINE FLYING AMONG THE STARS.
AND THAT'S THE END OF THE STORY. GOOD NIGHT, LITTLE LISTENER, SWEET DREAMS AND DON'T FORGET TO LOOK AT THE STARRY SKY EVERY NIGHT BEFORE YOU GO TO SLEEP!

The mouse Tino and the fox

ONCE UPON A TIME THERE WAS A LITTLE MOUSE NAMED TINO WHO LIVED IN A LITTLE HOUSE IN THE FIELDS. TINO LOVED TO PLAY AND RUN AROUND OUTSIDE, BUT EVERY NIGHT BEFORE HE WENT TO SLEEP, HE HAD TO DO ONE VERY IMPORTANT THING: CHECK THAT ALL HIS WINTER SUPPLIES WERE SAFE.
ONE DAY, WHILE TINO WAS CHECKING HIS SUPPLIES, HE MET AN OLD FOX WHO ASKED HIM IF HE NEEDED ANY HELP. TINO WAS VERY KIND, SO HE DECIDED TO SHARE HIS SUPPLIES WITH THE FOX.

THE NEXT NIGHT, TINO WOKE UP TO FIND THAT ALL HIS SUPPLIES WERE GONE. HE WAS VERY SAD AND THOUGHT THAT THE FOX HAD BEEN THE ONE TO STEAL THE FOOD. BUT WHEN HE WENT TO TALK TO THE FOX, HE FOUND OUT THAT IT WAS NOT SHE WHO HAD STOLEN IT, BUT A GROUP OF HUNGRY SQUIRRELS LIVING IN THE NEARBY WOODS.

TINO DECIDED TO HELP THE SQUIRRELS AND SHARE HIS FOOD WITH THEM. AND SO, WHEN WINTER CAME, ALL THE ANIMALS IN THE CAMP WERE SAFE AND HAD ENOUGH FOOD TO GET THROUGH THE COLD.

AND THAT'S THE END OF THE STORY. GOOD NIGHT, LITTLE LISTENER, SWEET DREAMS!

The adventure of the little unicorn

THE LITTLE UNICORN WAS ALWAYS CURIOUS AND DREAMED OF EXPLORING THE ENCHANTED FOREST BEYOND THE HILL. ONE DAY, HE DECIDED IT WAS TIME TO FULFILL HIS DREAM AND SET OFF ON HIS ADVENTURE. THE LITTLE UNICORN SET OFF ON HIS ADVENTURE, CROSSING THE GREEN FIELDS AND CRYSTAL CLEAR RIVERS. ON HIS JOURNEY, HE MET A FOX WHO WAS LOOKING FOR A SAFE PLACE TO HIDE HIS TREASURE. THE LITTLE UNICORN DECIDED TO HELP THE FOX AND TOGETHER THEY CONTINUED THEIR JOURNEY.
FINALLY, THE LITTLE UNICORN AND THE FOX ARRIVED AT THE ENCHANTED FOREST. IT WAS A PLACE FULL OF WONDERS AND MAGICAL CREATURES, SUCH AS FAIRIES, GOBLINS AND DRAGONS. THE LITTLE UNICORN AND THE FOX WERE EXCITED TO EXPLORE THIS ENCHANTED PLACE AND MET A RABBIT WHO JOINED THEM ON THEIR ADVENTURE.

WHILE EXPLORING THE FOREST, THE LITTLE UNICORN, FOX AND RABBIT MET THE FLOWER FAIRY, WHO GAVE THEM VALUABLE ADVICE. THE FAIRY TOLD THEM THAT THE DRAGON LIVING IN THE FOREST WAS CAUSING TROUBLE AND THAT ONLY A BRAVE HERO WOULD BE ABLE TO DEFEAT IT. THE LITTLE UNICORN, THE FOX AND THE RABBIT DECIDED THAT THEY WOULD MEET THE CHALLENGE AND DEFEAT THE DRAGON. THE LITTLE UNICORN, THE FOX AND THE RABBIT FACED THE DRAGON AND, DESPITE HIS FRIGHTENING FLAMES, WERE ABLE TO DEFEAT HIM WITH THE HELP OF THE FRIENDS THEY HAD MET ALONG THE WAY. THE DRAGON REALIZED THAT HE HAD DONE WRONG AND APOLOGIZED, PROMISING NOT TO CAUSE ANY MORE TROUBLE.

AS A REWARD FOR DEFEATING THE DRAGON, THE LITTLE UNICORN, THE FOX AND THE RABBIT RECEIVED AN ENCHANTED TREASURE

AFTER RECEIVING THE TREASURE, THE LITTLE UNICORN, THE FOX AND THE RABBIT DECIDED TO RETURN HOME. ON THEIR RETURN JOURNEY, THEY MET MANY OTHER ENCHANTED CREATURES WHO WANTED TO THANK THEM FOR DEFEATING THE DRAGON AND RESTORING PEACE TO THE ENCHANTED FOREST. WHEN THEY ARRIVED HOME, THE LITTLE UNICORN REALIZED THAT HIS ADVENTURE HAD TAUGHT HIM A GREAT LESSON. HE HAD LEARNED THAT FRIENDSHIP AND COURAGE CAN OVERCOME ANY OBSTACLE AND THAT, TOGETHER, ANYTHING IS POSSIBLE. AND SO, THE LITTLE UNICORN DECIDED TO SHARE THIS LESSON WITH ALL HIS FRIENDS IN THE MEADOW, HOPING THAT THEY, TOO, MIGHT ONE DAY EXPERIENCE A SIMILAR ADVENTURE.
AND SO, WITH A NEW UNDERSTANDING OF LIFE AND FRIENDSHIP, THE LITTLE UNICORN LIVES HAPPILY EVER AFTER.

Little Bear Bruno

ONCE UPON A TIME THERE WAS A LITTLE BEAR NAMED BRUNO WHO LIVED IN A BEAUTIFUL LITTLE HOUSE IN THE MIDDLE OF A FOREST. BRUNO LOVED PLAYING WITH HIS FOREST ANIMAL FRIENDS, SUCH AS THE FOX, RABBIT AND HERON.

BUT ONE DAY, BRUNO NOTICED THAT THE SUN WAS SETTING AND IT WAS TIME TO GO HOME TO SLEEP. AS HE WAS WALKING TO HIS LITTLE HOUSE, HE MET AN OWL WHO TOLD HIM, "BRUNO, THERE WILL BE A BIG STORM TONIGHT. YOU WILL BE SAFE IF YOU STAY AWAKE AND LOOK OUT THE WINDOW."

BRUNO WAS A LITTLE SCARED, BUT HE DECIDED TO BE BRAVE AND DO AS THE OWL ADVISED HIM. SO, HE GOT INTO BED AND STAYED AWAKE LISTENING TO THE THUNDER AND WATCHING THE STORM.

BUT IT WASN'T SCARY AT ALL! THE WIND WAS BLOWING HARD, BUT BRUNO WAS SAFE IN HIS LITTLE HOUSE, AND THE GUSTS OF WIND SANG HIM A SWEET LULLABY. THE LIGHTNING FLASHES LIT UP THE SKY, CREATING FANTASTIC SHAPES AND BRILLIANT COLORS. IT WAS A WONDERFUL SIGHT!

EVENTUALLY, THE STORM PASSED AND BRUNO FELL ASLEEP, HAPPY AND SAFE, DREAMING OF ALL THE BEAUTIFUL ADVENTURES HE WOULD HAVE IN THE WOODS THE NEXT DAY.

AND THAT'S THE END OF THE STORY. GOOD NIGHT, LITTLE LISTENER, SWEET DREAMS!

THANK YOU FOR LISTENING TO OUR STORIES,
SWEET DREAMS

Printed by
Libri Plureos GmbH · Friedensallee 273
22763 Hamburg · Germany